R
E
V
E
L
A
T
I
O
N

OF

CALVARY

Romel Duane Moore

Prayer Changes Things Publishing

Prayer Changes Things (PCT) Publishing
7551 Kingsport Road
Indianapolis, Indiana 46256

Scripture quotations, unless otherwise noted are from the King James Version of the Bible.

Cover design by Jan Taylor

Printed in the United States of America.

Edited by Dorothy Thompson and Margaret Rose Mejia.

ISBN 13: 978-1535360173
ISBN 10: 1535360178

The name satan is intentionally not capitalized.

CONTENTS

DEDICATION

This book is dedicated to those who hunger and thirst for the deeper things of God. Never apologize for this gift! "It is the glory of God to conceal a thing: but the honour of kings to search out a matter." *Proverbs 25:2*

INTRODUCTION

The purpose of this book is to unveil many of the mysteries pertaining to the place where Jesus was crucified and the things that happened to Him before and during the crucifixion. The mountain that He died upon was named "Place of the Skull" because it was a hill shaped like a man's head. Many Bible scholars believe it was also the original place where the headship of man fell in the Garden of Eden.

We will take a journey through the last days of Jesus' life and uncover some truths that will encourage and strengthen your faith beyond measure. If you are ready to feed your spirit with the meat of God's Word, then grab your Bible, concordance, pen, pad, and let's begin.

CHAPTER ONE

Fall and Redemption

For as by one man's disobedience many were made sinners, so by the obedience of one shall many be made righteous.

Romans 5:19

he Old Testament contains prophetic stories that retell the *Fall and Redemption of Man*. In the **Sixth Chapter of Second Kings** we see one of those stories. It begins with the account of Elisha and the iron that "swam." The location where the sons of the prophets were dwelling had become too small, so one of the prophets suggested that they move to Jordan and cut down wood to enlarge their dwelling place. Elisha agreed to this proposal, and they departed to accomplish the task when something very prophetic occurred. As one of the sons of the prophets was chopping down a tree, his axe head fell into the water, and he cried out, *"Alas, master! for it was borrowed."* **2Kings 6:5**

A borrowed axe was very expensive, and this frightened the young prophet because of the debt he would incur. Elisha asked him where the axe head fell and he showed Elisha the place. Elisha cut down a stick from a nearby tree and cast it where the young prophet said the axe head fell. Miraculously, the axe head began "to swim" and the prophet *"put out his hand, and took it."* **2Kings 6:7**

This story is a Old Testament picture of the *Fall and Redemption of Man*. It begins with a new building program, which represents the **First Two Chapters of Genesis**, when God restored the Earth and placed Adam and Eve in the Garden of Eden to be fruitful, multiply, and replenish the Earth. But as the sons of the prophets' building program began, the prophet's axe head fell into the water. This is a picture of the Fall of man's headship. The axe head in this story is symbolic of the headship of man over the Earth. When the prophet lost the axe head, he screamed that it was borrowed. The headship that was given to Adam was not his by ownership, but he was only a steward over it. God delegated the authority over the Earth to Adam, so it was not his to lose. When Adam and Eve ate from the forbidden tree, they lost their headship (the axe head fell into the water).

Because Adam and Eve sinned by eating from the *tree of the knowledge of good and evil*, it caused death to enter into the human race and with this a great debt because of their transgression. It was impossible for man to save himself, and the only deliverance for man would have to come from God. This is an interesting point. The debt that man owed was to God (He owned the axe head). So how could God be the one to pay the debt? This reveals the boundless love God has for man. God's holiness demanded that man die for his sins, but God's mercy demanded that God save man from His judgment of eternal death and separation from Him. ***Romans 6:23***

In addition, the son of the prophet was cutting down a tree when his axe *head* fell into the water. First, Adam and Eve ate from a tree when they lost their *headship* over the Earth. Thus, it was a tree that got man in trouble, and it would take a tree to get him out of trouble. When Elisha asked the man where the axe *head* fell, he went to a tree, cut down a stick, threw it into the water at the exact location where the axe *head* fell and then it began to miraculously swim so the young prophet could "pick it up." This story is symbolic of the *Fall and Redemption of Mankind*. The place where Adam's *headship* fell would be the same place where Christ (the last Adam) would pick it back up. Elisha cut down a stick and God cut down a stick, called the Cross. Jesus, the last Adam, didn't carry His cross to any location, but it was the exact location where the first Adam's *headship* fell.

Fruit is what hangs on a tree and Adam and Eve ate the fruit from a tree. Jesus hung on the tree of the Cross and today we are able to come and eat from *the tree of life* that His death, burial and resurrection gives fruit. The *headship* of man over planet Earth has been restored because God cast the stick of the Cross to the same place the axe *head* fell in the Garden of Eden. This is why the hill that Jesus died upon is called the "Place of a Skull" because it is the same place the *headship* and authority of man fell.

Because the fallen axe *head* debt had to be paid, when Jesus died for man's sin, He became man's sacrifice and paid the sin debt that was owed. This event appeased the necessary judgment that God's holiness required for the sins of man, and it also restored man back to his original place as the *head* of God's creation. All we have to do is "put out our hand and take it up."[1]

Divine Intervention

The ***Fourth Chapter of Second Kings*** records the story of the Prophet Elisha and a great Shunammite woman. This woman's husband was old and past childbearing years. Anytime Elisha and his servant Gehazi would pass through their city, the Shunammite woman and her husband were very hospitable to them. As a result of this kindness, the Prophet Elisha told her that by a certain time the following year she would give birth to a son and that's exactly what happened. Some years later, the child was a young man, and one day as he went out to meet his father in the field with the reapers, calamity hit him. He cried out to his father, *"My head, my head,"* and shortly after the child died. No one knows

A Revelation of Calvary

exactly what was wrong with him except that the pain came from his head.

The young man died on his mother's lap, and she placed him on the bed that she prepared for the Prophet Elisha during his many visits to their home. She went to Mount Carmel to tell Elisha of her misfortune, believing if God used Elisha to help bring about the miracle of his birth, then God would also use Elisha to bring about a miracle to raise him from the dead.

Elisha's servant, Gehazi, was sent ahead of them with instructions from Elisha to place his staff on the face of the dead body, hoping it might revive him, but it did not. When Elisha arrived, he entered the room where the young man lay dead and Elisha laid upon him and *"put his mouth upon his mouth, and his eyes upon his eyes, and his hands upon his hands: and he stretched himself upon the child." 2Kings 4:34* He then left the room and walked in the house "to and fro" and went back up to the room and laid upon the boy again, but this time the boy sneezed seven times and opened his eyes.

11

This story is another picture of the *Fall and Redemption* of man. The Prophet Elisha is a type of Christ, and the miracle birth of the Shunammite woman's son represents mankind. The Word of God gave us life. Our problems and ultimate death came by the words *"My head, my head."* As we work the mission field of this fallen world, out preaching the Gospel and laboring with the "reapers," the birth of the carnal mind that came when Adam and Eve ate from the *tree of the knowledge of good and evil*, is what causes our demise every time. Since then, every form of death can be linked back to that formidable day when we lost our headship in the Garden of Eden.

God created man to serve as the head of the planet. He desired that man would rule Earth the way He rules Heaven, but we lost our headship when Adam disobeyed in the Garden of Eden. There was nothing man could do in this unregenerate state to save himself, so we entered a perpetual state of death. The sending of Elisha's servant, Gehazi, with the staff to lay on the dead boy was symbolic of God sending His servant, Moses, with his staff as the lawgiver. Moses gave man God's laws. Although the law is righteous and just, it could not save, redeem, or revive man. The law was given to reveal to man how sinful and corrupt he truly is and that without Divine intervention, man could never be saved.

The coming of Elisha from Mount Carmel (meaning *plenty*) is a type of Christ leaving the palatial halls of Heaven in order to come to Earth to redeem man. This was the purpose of Elisha laying upon the dead boy with *"his mouth upon his mouth, and his eyes upon his eyes, and his hands upon his hands; and he stretched himself upon the child."* In other words, Christ came in the form of man. He looked like us. He had eyes, hands, and a mouth like us. The Word was made flesh and dwelt among us.

As Elisha walked "to and fro" represents how Jesus walked thirty-three and a half years upon this Earth just like you and I. He knows how we feel and how we emote. He is one hundred percent God and one hundred percent man. When His mission was fulfilled as a man, He went back up to the Upper Room where the dead body lay (man dead in sins) in the form of the Calvary's Cross that was suspended between Heaven and Earth. As a man now, having touched and experienced the same things we have, He became sin for us. But this time as he "lied upon the child" the child sneezed seven times and opened his eyes. Sneezing is the quickest form of an orgasm. The boy sneezing seven times represents the resurrection of Christ from the dead and man's ultimate redemption. Christ's death restored intimacy and fellowship between man and God. He destroyed the enmity that lingered because of man's sin. Because of Calvary, man can enter into the Presence of God again. The seven sneezes represent perfect or complete intimacy with God. Christ was willing to leave Mount Carmel (type of Heaven) and humble Himself to our low estate. He placed his eyes upon our eyes, and his hands upon our hands, and his mouth upon our mouth, and became flesh. Now our eyes can be opened from the curse of sin and the carnal mind; and we can enjoy the benefits of being restored back to intimacy with God and headship.

CHAPTER TWO
Ram in the Bush

Your father Abraham rejoiced to see my day: and he saw it, and was glad.

Then said the Jews unto him, Thou are not yet fifty years old, and hast thou seen Abraham?

Jesus said unto them, Verily, verily, I say unto you, Before Abraham was, I am.

John 8:56-58

*J*esus was in a heated exchange with the Jews concerning their relationship with God through the Patriarch, Abraham. Not realizing that the Son of God was in their midst, they debated with Jesus based on Abraham being their father. The Lord's final response that ultimately caused them to take up stones to attempt to kill Him, was that Abraham *"rejoiced to see His day: and he saw it, and was glad."* He told them, *"Before Abraham was,*

15

I am." Claiming the Almighty Title of "I Am" made Him God and this was not acceptable to their ears. I would like to pose the question. When did Abraham rejoice to see Jesus day and when did he see it and was glad? Let's look at *Genesis 22:13-14*:

And Abraham lifted up his eyes, and looked, and behold behind him a ram caught in a thicket by his horns: and Abraham went and took the ram, and offered him up for a burnt offering in the stead of his son.

And Abraham called the name of that place Jehovah jireh: as it is said to this day, In the mount of the Lord it shall be seen.

Most of us know the story of when God told Abraham to offer up Isaac, his son. He made Isaac carry the wood for his own death up Mount Moriah. We understand this to be a foreshadow of Jesus carrying the Cross of Calvary to His own death. Abraham about to sacrifice his son, was the type of God who was sacrificing Jesus for mankind. What we probably missed was the fact that Abraham not only received the sacrificial substitute for Isaac in the form of the ram caught in the thicket, but also when He initially "lifted up his eyes, and looked" was when God allowed him to see what Jesus called His day and was glad.

When Abraham "lifted up his eyes, and looked...behind him," he was actually seeing in front of him. He saw in front of him, the future, because this is when he saw Jesus fifteen hundred years in the future on Calvary giving His life for the sins of man. Why does the Bible say Abraham saw behind him if he really saw the future? The Bible says that Jesus was the "Lamb slain from (before) the foundation of the world." *Revelation 13:8* Although Calvary wouldn't take place for another fifteen hundred years, according to God it already happened.

God does not live in time, but time lives in Him. Time consists of three dimensions: past, present and future. God is so big that all three dimensions of time live in Him at the same time. This is why Jesus said, "I am Alpha and Omega, the beginning and the end, the first and the last." *Revelation 22:13* Abraham was looking behind him, and saw in front of him, and it was the same event because Jesus is the beginning and the end.

Ram in the Thicket

What Abraham lifted up his eyes to behold was a "ram caught in a thicket." A ram is a mature male sheep with horns. The ram that Abraham saw had its horns "caught in a thicket." A thicket is a bush of thorns and thistles entwined. This ram whose horns were caught in a thicket was actually Jesus (the Lamb of God) wearing a crown of thorns given to Him by the Roman soldiers on Golgotha's hill. God allowed Abraham to see this event supernaturally, and this is what Jesus was referring to when he said, "Abraham rejoiced to see His day and he saw it, and was glad." Abraham rejoiced when he saw Jesus dying on Calvary because he understood that what God had asked of him in sacrificing his son, Isaac, was only the precursor to Christ's ultimate fulfillment.

Ram's Horn

Abraham saw a ram with its horns caught in a bush of thorns. We cannot overlook that it was the ram's horns caught in the thicket, not its leg or tail. To fully understand this, let's see what horns represent and what ram's horns were used for in those days. Horns represent strength and power. When two rams are in conflict, they fight with their horns. Many times the strength of their horns determines the victor.

Inside the Inner Court of the Tabernacle of Moses was a piece of furniture called the Altar of Incense. Attached to this altar were rams' horns and incense that the priest burned continually. This burning incense represents the prayers of the saints which should be fiery and hot (*James 5:16* says, "The effectual fervent prayer of a righteous man availeth much). The beautiful fragrance of the incense represents how our fiery prayers smell to God and fill Heaven's atmosphere. As the smoke of the incense rose in the inner court, the prayers of the saints ascend to Heaven.

19

The rams' horns connected to the Altar of Incense symbolize the strength of our prayers. Our prayers are strong because we know God hears us. Our prayers have power because we speak to mountains to be removed and cast into the sea and God does it. Our prayers are strong because we have a High Priest that is touched with the feeling of our infirmities (*Hebrews 4:15*) and makes intercession for us (day and night). *Romans 8:34* The main reason horns represent the strength of our prayers is because something had to die in order for the horns to be used. The beginning of God is at the end of us. And when we are no longer in the way, God's will can be done and His Kingdom can come on Earth as it is in Heaven.

Also, ram's horns were used as containers for the anointing oil. We desire to be containers or vessels that carry the anointing of the Holy Ghost. But are we willing to die to self, give our life, in order for our horns to be used for God's glory? Will we disconnect from relationships that are not going in the direction God has us going? Can we fast, pray, study, sacrifice and consecrate our lives to the degree where we establish the right kind of relationship with God where He can pour into us His wisdom, knowledge and Spirit?

Furthermore, ram's horns were used as trumpets. The sound of the trumpet gave instructions to the people. If they blew the trumpets a certain way, the people knew the enemy was near and to prepare for war. If they blew the trumpet another way, it instructed the people to assemble together. If God does not have our horns, He cannot use us to warn, instruct or encourage others. God does not call the qualified, but He qualifies those He calls, and we are called to take up our cross and follow Him.

When Abraham saw the ram with its horns caught in the thicket, he supernaturally saw Jesus fifteen hundred years later, wearing the crown of thorns for the sins of man. It was the ram's horns caught in the thicket because the horns are attached to the head and it was not an easy decision for Jesus when it was time to die for us. In Gethsemane, Christ agonized in His soul until He sweated great drops of Blood. In order for one's pupils to dilate large enough for blood to pass though means the person is in so much pain, they are on the brink of

21

death. An angel had to strengthen Jesus, and He had to pray three times before the reality of the crucifixion was settled in Jesus' mind. Abraham witnessed this struggle as the ram (Jesus) had its horns (Jesus' head) caught in the thicket (thorns). Abraham rejoiced when he witnessed this event supernaturally and he was glad!

Mount Moriah

The mountain that God instructed Abraham to offer Isaac upon was called Mt. Moriah. This mountain is not identified today if you were to visit the Holy Land. *Genesis 22:14* says, *"In the mount of the Lord it shall be seen." (redemption)* God called Mount Moriah the Mount of the Lord. Mount Calvary is the Mount of the Lord because this is where the Lord gave His life for us. Many scholars believe that Mount Moriah in Abraham's day was Mount Calvary in Jesus' day. Abraham looked behind him and saw the past which was really the future, while he was standing in the present at the identical location where the event would take place.

CHAPTER THREE
Don't Sweat It

And being in an agony he prayed more earnestly: and his sweat was as it were great drops of blood falling down to the ground.
Luke 22:44

Jesus had just entered into what we affectionately call His Passion or suffering. After the Last Supper with His twelve disciples, Jesus knew Judas would be the one to betray Him and sent him away with the words, "That thou doest, do quickly." *John 13:27* They left the Upper Room scene of the Last Supper and came to the secluded location of the Garden of Gethsemane. It was here that Jesus began to agonize over the great sufferings that laid ahead of Him in order to save humanity from sins. The Bible says, "without shedding of blood is no remission (of sins.)" *Hebrews 9:22* The first place Jesus shed His innocent Blood was from His

23

head as *"his sweat was as it were great drops of blood falling down to the ground."*

Christ's head was the first place where Blood was shed. This did not happen by accident, but God was revealing some very powerful truths to us concerning our redemption. We have discovered so far that man's redemption was connected to headship. We've discussed the Shunammite son who said, *"My head, my head,"* before he died. We also discussed the significance of the ram's horn that was caught in the thicket during Abraham's visit to Mount Moriah, and the axe head that fell during the time of Elisha. The Fall of man had everything to do with the Fall of his headship. But not just his headship concerning delegated authority, but also the condition of his mind after the Fall.

The Curse of Sweat

Christ came to redeem us from the curse of poverty, sickness, and death. The only substance on Earth that can remit sin is blood, so when Jesus began to *sweat* Blood it pointed to the curse that was instituted after the Fall in the Garden of Eden.

In the sweat of thy face shalt thou eat bread, till thou return unto the ground . . . **Genesis 3:19**

Immediately after the Fall of man, God began to explain the curses that had come about because of man's disobedience. Eve was cursed with pain during childbearing. Satan was cursed with the prophecy of the seed of the woman bruising his head. **Genesis 3:15** Adam was cursed with the result of *sweat* as he toiled on Earth. **Genesis 3:19** This might seem insignificant at first glance, but if the curse was *sweat*, then this means that before the Fall, God intended for man to be able to work without feeling pain resulting in *sweat*. **Ezekiel**

44:18 instructs the priesthood not to wear any clothing that would cause them to *sweat*.

When a person *sweats*, the first part of the body that it appears is on the head. *Sweat* was a result of the curse, so it would be the first area Christ shed Blood to remit man's sin. Jesus *sweat* Blood so we wouldn't have to sweat the different effects that the Fall caused our minds to go through, such as depression, anxiety, worry, suicide, stress, mental illnesses, and personality disorders. Christ's Blood redeemed us from all these harmful affects, and it is our job to understand this truth and use it as a defense when we start to lose our peace of mind.

Hebrews 9:14 says the Blood of Jesus is able to *"purge your conscience from dead works to serve the living God."* Did you know that because Jesus *sweat* Blood we don't have to *sweat* insomnia? We have a covenant right to get good sleep at night. The things that disturb our thoughts and imagination is covered under the Blood of Jesus and rest is ours to have. We don't have to take any of the over-the-counter drugs to aid us to sleep at night. Take the Word of God and apply it to your life. When I can't sleep, I say aloud, "Jesus *sweat* Blood so I wouldn't have to *sweat* insomnia. In the Name of Jesus, Lord, you promised to give your beloved rest. I thank you now that I will sleep like a baby this night!"

Jesus wouldn't have had to *sweat* Blood if man didn't have a head problem. Long before we sin with our body, we first sin with our mind. What we don't like to deal with, are the sins of our imagination. What we do, is the fruit of sin, and why we do it, is the root of sin. We would rather put a temporary bandage on cancer than go through the pain of chemotherapy or radiation that is needed to destroy the cancer at its root. Jesus said that one does not sin when he lies with someone to fornicate, but his sin began when he lusted for the person in his or her heart (*Matthew 5:28*).

Man has many sins of the imagination like envy, jealousy, doubt, disbelief, worry, fear, prejudice, fantasies, lust, masturbation, anger, and malice. Much of our mental contemplation is the misuse of our mind. When someone angers us, we visually rehearse cursing or hurting him or her, though we might not ever go through with it. When we get a pain in our body, we mentally converse with ourselves and claim a thousand diseases we think may be the cause of the pain, when nothing has been diagnosed.

Crowning Point

The body does what the mind tells it to do. If our mind is diseased, the rest of the body will be diseased. If the mind is healthy, the rest of the body will be healthy. When a baby is being delivered, the most important obstacle the midwife must overcome is called "the crowning point." In order to have a successful birth, the head of the child must come out first. If an arm or leg comes out first, there is a possibility of death for the baby and the mother. But once the head is properly aligned and breaches the womb first, the midwife can take a huge sigh of relief because she knows that if the head is okay (crowning point), the rest of the body will be also.

We can go through things that seem to snuff the very life from us. Separation, divorce, death, broken relationships, abuse, strife, and schisms can all add to the destruction of our mental well-being. God has not left us comfortless. When Blood dropped from Jesus' head, He was not only relating to our agony, but He was redeeming us from everything that would violate our peace of mind.

If satan can successfully get our heads messed up, he knows that he has already won the battle because the body is sure to follow the thoughts of our minds. If our minds are depressed we will not be able to function at full capacity in other areas of our lives. If we allow broken relationships to open the door to mental illnesses, it is inevitable for the rest of our lives to become ill. The head isn't just the location of the mind, but also the eyes, ears, nose and mouth.

When we think improperly, it will affect our vision, hearing, discernment, and the words we speak. When Jesus *sweat* Blood from His head, He was redeeming us from every mental malfunction, everything that would take our peace of mind, every fear and anxiety known to man. Each time someone we loved cursed at us, it triggered something in our minds. When the teacher told us we were stupid and would never be anything, it twisted something emotionally. When we suffered physical abuse, sexual abuse, and verbal abuse, it rearranged the proper alignment we once enjoyed when we came through our mother's womb. When our mind is "getting the best of us," just remember that Jesus *sweat* Blood so that we wouldn't have to *sweat*. Don't *sweat* it!

CHAPTER FOUR

Crown of Thorns

And they clothed him with purple, and platted a crown of thorns, and put it about his head.

Mark 15:17

One of the cruel acts that Jesus had to endure during His Passion was the placing of the crown of thorns upon His head. This was done to mock Him since He said that He was the King of the Jews. What the soldiers did not know was that they were doing something very prophetic that would continually bring redemption and healing for the mind of man. We learned in the previous chapter that *sweat* was a part of the curse when man fell; now let's look at what part thorns played in the curse also.

31

. . . cursed is the ground for thy sake; in sorrow shalt thou eat of it all the days of thy life;

thorns also and thistles shall it bring forth to thee; and thou shalt eat the herb of the field.

Genesis 3:17-18

Another result of the Fall of man was the curse of the ground and that it would produce thorns and thistles as man attempted to live off the land. Thorns are a very prickly plant that can grow just about anywhere. In ancient times, farmers used thorns as a fence to keep rodents from wasting their produce. This was called a "thorn-hedge." In the *Parable of the Sower*, one of the four types of man's heart was called "thorns." *Matthew 13:7* says, *"And some fell among thorns; and the thorns sprung up, and choked them."*

Jesus said that when your heart is a "thorny" heart, it will choke the seed of the Word of God that's sown within it. We wonder why it's so hard to bear good fruit from all the Word of God we ingest. The many Bible Studies, Sunday School Lessons, Sunday Sermons, books, tapes, CDs, DVDs and Livestreams that we consume each year should leave us in better condition than we are, but the Word cannot do us any good if our hearts are not right. The problem is never the Word of God. His Word is always alive, powerful, wholesome, and full of potential. It is the thorns in our hearts that come from our minds that continue to spring up and choke the potential of God's Word within us.

Thorns in Your Side

But if ye will not drive out the inhabitants of the land from before you; then it shall come to pass, that those which ye let remain of them shall be pricks in your eyes, and thorns in your sides, and shall vex you in the land wherein ye dwell.

Numbers 33:55

God reminded Israel over and over about the danger of allowing strange nations to dwell among them with their false gods and idols, because they would become pricks in their eyes, thorns in their sides, and would vex them. The inhabitants that we allow to remain in our land today that can become pricks, thorns, and vexations, are the baggage we pick up from our broken homes, the abuse we endured from family members or intimate relationships, the anger we acquired from dwelling in a dysfunctional home, the drug addiction and abnormal behavior acquired along the way in life.

The Bible says that these inhabitants would be thorns in our sides. Imagine having to walk around with something very sharp piercing your rib cage, and there was nothing you could do about it. Apostle Paul experienced this when he prayed three times, asking God to deliver him from a "thorn in the flesh." He called this thorn in the flesh a messenger from satan sent to buffet him. Whenever we don't deal with past circumstances, mental issues and emotional baggage, we are permitting these alien inhabitants to live, thrive, and reproduce within our lives.

When someone experiences the bitterness of a broken heart and does not get the proper counseling, prayer and healing, they are setting their next relationship up for failure because we have a biblical mandate to kick out the inhabitants in our land that will become pricks, thorns, and vexations. When we are not totally healed from past relationships and circumstances, we become prey to the offspring those dark seasons produce and leave behind like resentment, rejection, anger, malice, and strife.

Bishop Veron Ashe said, *"Ninety percent of our problems today is ourselves left-over from yesterday."* The first step to healing is admitting that we have a problem. There are multiplied millions of people walking the Earth with serious mental and emotional issues, but they think that they are okay. God cannot fix us if we don't recognize we need fixing and ask Him to do it.

We are raising our families, working our jobs, going to our perspective places of worship, all while suffering from "stinking thinking," lack of common sense, bad understanding, emotional imbalances, and irrational or illogical thinking. On top of this, we expect others to accept us, and tolerate our pricks, thorns and vexations without an argument. Whatever we call normal, we are not able to change, but others can see our abnormality much easier than we can. However, they aren't as quick to give residence to the offspring we picked up from yesterday's dysfunction.

Carnal Mind

The tree that man ate from that caused man's Fall was called *the tree of the knowledge of good and evil*. When Adam and Eve tasted the fruit from this tree, the Bible records that their eyes were opened and *"they knew that they were naked." **Genesis 3:7*** I believe this was the birth of the carnal mind in man. One tree had two knowledges called good and evil. This lets us know that something or someone can be good, but produces death at the same time. It is very important that we get this truth. Just because something is perceived to be good doesn't mean it will produce life, it can still produce death.

The carnal mind is the product of this tree of two knowledges (double-minded). The carnal mind is more than thinking on carnal things like lust and greed, but it is our unnatural need to categorize everything we experience under *good* or *evil*. For instance, when we get a promotion on our job, we automatically label that as *good*, and when we are fired or laid off from our employer, we automatically label that experience as *evil*.

After some time has passed and we are able to see in hindsight, many times we see that what we called *good* was actually *evil* and what we called *evil* was actually *good*.

Maybe the promotion required longer hours at the job that took you away from your family, church and quiet time with God. Maybe being fired from one position freed you up to pursue your dream of starting your own business. It is the carnal mind that drives us to categorize every situation as *good* or *evil*, because the carnal mind must be able to figure out, calculate, "size-up," understand, intellectualize, label, and give an instant verdict about whatever we encounter.

We can attend a church service and leave there, saying in our mind, "The pastor really preached today, and the anointing was strong." We come to this conclusion because the service was more emotional than usual, and the response from the people was positive. Perhaps the next church service isn't as emotional, and the pastor spoke about some hard-hitting issues and the people's response was a bit more lukewarm. We leave there, saying, "Today wasn't as good as last week. I wish the pastor preached like he did before." Maybe the pastor preached what he was supposed to preach, exactly how he was supposed to preach it, but since one message didn't make your flesh feel good and the other one did, the carnal mind labeled it as *good* and *evil*. **Romans 8:6-7** records:

For to be carnally minded is death; but to be spiritually minded is life and peace.

Because the carnal mind is enmity against God: for it is not subject to the law of God, neither indeed can be.

We know from Scripture that satan and his angels are enemies of God, but we never consider that the way we think can position us as enemies of God. The carnal mind is God's enemy, and the Bible says it *"is enmity against God,"* which means it is hatred with God. For instance, when we meet someone that is supposed to be a man or woman of God, and just because they don't dress the way our ingenious mind tells us that a man or woman of God is supposed to dress or talk, walk, and act how our "holy roller selves" say is appropriate, the carnal mind instantly sizes them up and spits out the verdict of "false, not real, impersonator." Death is not just the expiration of life in one's body, but Paul explained (to be carnally minded is death) that death is the way we can think. You can have five degrees on the wall and still be dead. You can have a ten thousand-member church and be dead. You can be the most successful man or woman materially walking the Earth, but because you are carnally minded, God says you are dead.

Crown of Thorns

When the crown of thorns was brutally placed on the Lord's head, it did more than give Him excruciating pain, it was delivering us from the curse of the carnal mind, the thorns of every negative emotion, every feeling and thought that vexes us, every mental illness, emotional imbalance that keeps us stuck in seasons, and every sin of the imagination. When the Blood flowed from Christ's brow caused by the crown of thorns, Jesus was taking upon Himself the curse of the carnal mind that was birthed in the Garden of Eden. The Fall produced the curse of thorns, and Christ wore the thorns so we wouldn't have to. Thorns choke the Word of God

39

from the hearts of man, and Jesus was delivering us from the effects of a "thorny" heart that will never allow us to fully produce the fruit of God's Word.

This means we don't have to sit back and passively tolerate the abnormal conditions of our hearts and minds. Christ sweat Blood so that we wouldn't have to sweat depression, fear, and doubt. Christ wore the crown of thorns so we wouldn't have to suffer the affects of the thorns that choke the Word. We don't have to have personality disorders. We don't have to suffer mental illnesses. We don't have to be depressed, suicidal, or one click away from a mental asylum.

The greatest weapon the church has in its awesome arsenal is the Blood of Jesus. Jesus' Blood is the only means by which we can be forgiven and saved. As He sweat Blood from His head in Gethsemane and shed Blood from His head by the crown of thorns, He was leaving an irrefutable legacy for us that says that we have been redeemed from the curse of every known mental, emotional, and psychological defect, disease, and illness.

It is our mind that is sick. It's our mind that is diseased. We go through life like the Shunammite son who yelled, *"My head, my head."* God knows the condition of our heads and He made covenant provisions specifically for this problem through our Lord and Savior Jesus Christ. As Robert Lowry, the songwriter of old wrote, *"What can wash away my sins? Nothing but the Blood of Jesus. What can make me whole again? Nothing but the Blood of Jesus!"*[2]

CHAPTER FIVE
The Place of a Skull

And they bring him unto the place Golgotha, which is, being interpreted, The place of a skull.

Mark 15:22

The final stage of Jesus' death would be played out on a hill named Golgotha. What we must ask ourselves is this question: "Why this hill?" Jesus could have been crucified anywhere near Jerusalem. Why this hill named in the Hebrew tongue, Golgotha? God is not the kind of person who runs from a fight and when the first Adam sinned and lost headship over the planet that was delegated to him, God was not going to stop until Christ, the Second Adam, came to restore it.

Golgotha means *skull.* Another name for the hill Christ died upon is *the place of a skull.* The name Calvary is the Greek word *kranion* that means, *a skull.* It's where we get the English word, *cranium,* which is a man's head. This hill is believed to be the location where the Garden of Eden once existed, where the first Adam sinned and lost his headship. Therefore, it is not a coincidence that God orchestrated the hill of Jesus' crucifixion to be in the exact location where man's headship needed to be restored.

To make this point even stronger, this same hill happened to be shaped like a man's head. There is no doubt that God was trying to get us to understand that the *Crucifixion* and *Redemption of Man* was all about headship.

The Gardens

God always does things in threes: Abraham, Isaac, and Jacob; Outer court, Inner court, and Most Holy Place; thirty, sixty, and one hundred-fold; good, acceptable, and perfect will of God. God told Adam that the day he ate from the forbidden tree he would surely die, and this death was threefold because man is a tripartite being consisting of spirit, soul, and body. Adam died spiritually instantly after he ate, as he was spiritually disconnected from God. Adam inherited the carnal mind (which is death) as his soul slowly died, and finally Adam physically died.

Since man fell in a garden, when God was ready to redeem man, He wouldn't only do it in three stages, but He would do it in three gardens. First, in the Garden of Gethsemane, Jesus' soul was in great agony unto death. When He sweat great drops of Blood, He was redeeming the soul of man.

Second, as Jesus hung from the Cross, the thief on His right side said, *"...remember me when thou comest into thy kingdom."* And Jesus' response to Him was, *"To day shalt thou be with me in paradise."* **Luke 23:43** Paradise was the Garden of Eden. The Garden of Eden had been translated to the middle part of the Earth also called "Abraham's bosom" or "Hades." He died and went to the original Garden of Eden called "Paradise" to perform what the Bible says, *"...he led captivity captive and gave gifts unto men."* **Ephesians 4:8** This completed the *Redemption of Man* spiritually.

Third, the tomb that Jesus was buried in that belonged to the rich man Joseph of Arimathea, was in a garden. This is why on Resurrection Sunday, Mary Magdalene thought Jesus was the gardener. *John 20:15* Today, the location of Jesus' tomb is called "The Garden Tomb." God placed the first Adam in the Garden of Eden and told him to keep it. On Resurrection Sunday, the Second Adam was mistaken for a gardener. When God resurrected Jesus from the dead, the Bible says that the graves of the Saints were also opened and the Saints of old walked in Jerusalem. *Matthew 27: 52-53* When Jesus stepped out of the tomb and into a garden, it completed the *Redemption of Man* and the promise that one day we would receive glorified bodies. Man fell in a garden, and man was redeemed in three gardens.

Leave and Cleave

Therefore shall a man leave his father and his mother, and shall cleave unto his wife: and they shall be one flesh.

Genesis 2:24

When we read these words spoken by Adam after God presented Eve to him, we automatically think that Adam was speaking concerning the marital covenant between a husband and wife, but further investigation will reveal that this was not the case. Adam didn't have a mother and had no knowledge of being able to leave his mother and father. Adam was, in effect, prophesying about a future event. Apostle Paul picks this up where Adam left off in *Ephesians 5:31-32.*

For this cause shall a man leave his father and mother, and shall be joined unto his wife, and they two shall be one flesh.

This is a great mystery: but I speak concerning Christ and the church.

Paul quotes the words of the first Adam and says that it's been a great mystery the entire time, because those words were concerning the Second Adam, Christ, and His Church. If something is a mystery, it means the true understanding has not been revealed. Adam was prophesying about an event that would take place four thousand years later on Calvary. While hanging from the Cross, Jesus began the fulfillment of the mysterious words of Adam when He states in *John 19:26-27*:

When Jesus therefore saw his mother, and the disciple standing by, whom he loved, he saith unto his mother, Woman, behold thy son!

Then saith he to the disciple, Behold thy mother! And from that hour that disciple took her unto his own home.

Jesus told His Mother Mary that John would now become her new son and He told his Disciple John that Mary would now be his new mother. The Bible says that from that hour, John took Mary to his own home. Therefore, Jesus had fulfilled the words spoken by Adam concerning leaving His mother. When Jesus became sin for man, God could not look upon Him, and this is when Jesus cried out, *"My God, my God, why hast thou forsaken me?"* **Matthew 27:46** This fulfilled the prophecy of Christ leaving His father.

After He died, a Roman soldier pierced Him in the side. This mirrors the place where God put Adam to sleep and opened up his side and took a rib out in order to make Eve. When they pierced Jesus in the side, Blood and water came out. Blood and water are the elements of a human birth. Christ left his mother and Father and was now preparing to give birth to His Bride so He could cleave to His Wife.

Till Death Do Us Part

Jesus spoke explicitly, saying that the only way out of the marital covenant was by death. In our traditional marital vows we state at the end, "Till death do us part." Throughout the Old Testament, God referred to Israel as His Bride. Two thousand years ago, the Groom came to Earth in the flesh and walked with His bride. He taught her, healed her, delivered her, and comforted her, but she didn't receive Him and ultimately crucified Him. In doing so, she annulled their covenant. Because her Husband left the grave in three days, He was now free to choose for Himself a new Bride.

Because the Roman soldier pierced His side after He was put to sleep, He rose again on the third day with His Bride, fresh from Paradise and having the freedom to include the Gentiles from every tongue, race and culture as a part of His Bride. For the last two thousand years, Jesus has been cleaving to His Bride and becoming One Flesh. We are now "bone of His Bone and flesh of His Flesh!"

CHAPTER SIX
The Mind of Christ

But the Comforter, which is the Holy Ghost, whom the Father will send in my name, he shall teach you all things, and bring all things to your remembrance, whatsoever I have said unto you.

John 14:26

ave you ever had the feeling of "deja vu?" Have you ever stopped yourself in your tracks and said, "Man, I feel like I've been at this place before?" Have you ever met someone for the first time and said, "I feel like I've met this person before, and I've known him or her my entire life?" These feelings are a great reminder to us that before we were formed in our mother's womb, God knew us, sanctified us and ordained us (*Jeremiah 1:5*). Our beginning didn't begin when our birth began, but we were with God before the foundation of the world.

Jesus stated in the above Scripture in the **Book of John** that the Father would send the Holy Ghost and the Holy Ghost would bring all things to our remembrance of whatsoever He said to us. We may think this statement was referring strictly to the disciples standing before Him, but Jesus was speaking to all His disciples, present and future. Before we came through our mother's birth canal, we were in the Bosom of God. He showed us our life, our sufferings, our purpose, our destiny, and we said "yes" to being born in this fallen world. Upon our natural birth, we lost all knowledge of our past existence. Once we are born again in this life, the process by which we begin to remember certain things begins.

Amnesia

Amnesia is the loss of memory usually caused by trauma to the head. The Fall of Adam and loss of his headship was the head blow that caused each of us to be born into this world with "amnesia." When someone suffer from amnesia, they can't remember their identity. They can't recall their name, age, family or residence.

When Adam ate from the forbidden tree, he caused all of humanity to suffer a powerful blow to the head(ship), and we are now born into this world without being able to remember our true identity. We are ignorant about the relationship we had with God before time began. We have no knowledge of our real home, family, and name. It is not until we are born again that our amnesia begins to be healed, as the Spirit of Truth slowly brings all things and all truth to our remembrance. The Spirit of God is the Person Who causes us to recall our purpose, identity, name and spiritual family.

As we begin to study the Bible, God's Spirit shows us something we've never seen before. We call it *revelation*, but the word *revelation* lets us know that what was seen was not seen for the first time, but rather "revealed." Jesus said that the Holy Ghost would remind of us of all things that Christ said to us. When we receive *revelation knowledge*, we are simply being reminded of something Christ told us before the worlds were formed, not something explained to us for the first time. Our natural eyes from our natural birth are born into a fallen physical house called *flesh*. This *flesh* covers or veils us from what we once experienced and knew, so when God shows it to us, it isn't an unveiling (as if for the first time), but a revealing.

Circumcision

Circumcision is the surgical removal of the foreskin from around the head of the male sex organ. God instituted it through the Patriarch Abraham. God said that circumcision is the token (sign) of the covenant with Him. So when a Jewish male was circumcised, it symbolized the covenant he had with God.

When we accept the Lord into our lives, He lives inside of us as the Head of the Body of Christ. When we repent, we ask Christ to be the Head of our lives. But it is not enough for Jesus to live in us, His ultimate goal is to live through us. At this stage we are in need of circumcision. God desires to remove the carnal, fleshly, "earthy," fallen part of us that covers the true Headship. *Ephesians* tells us that the Sword of the Spirit is the Word of God. *The Book of Hebrews* instruct us that the Word of God is quick, powerful and shaper than any double-edged sword. As we submit to the teachings of

God's Word, His Spirit uses the Word as a Sword to systematically cut away at the flesh of our fallen nature, the flesh that veils the Headship of Jesus in our lives.

The foreskin is unclean and so is the flesh or carnal mind. The head is already present on the male sex organ, there's just skin hiding it. The Headship of Christ is present in the Christian life; the covering of carnality is hiding Him. We have the mind of Christ. We have the wisdom, understanding and will of Jesus, but our old man of the flesh is what continually veils Him from being seen and coming forth.

When a male has just been circumcised, the head of the sex organ is not use to the exposure and it is very sensitive to its surroundings. When a Christian is circumcised, the Headship of Christ is revealed and their life becomes very sensitive because of His compassion, mercy, love and selflessness. Jesus is the reason why we consider our brother before ourselves. He is why we love unconditionally. The Presence of His Headship causes us to be moved with compassion and touched with the feelings of other's infirmities. Circumcision reveals the head, and the Head of every Christian is Jesus.

Renew Your Mind

Everything we learn about the Word of God isn't the first time we heard it. We are being reminded. God is bringing it to our remembrance. "**Re**" is a prefix that means *to go back.* We cannot **re**deem something unless we first owned it. Once we lose what we first owned, we are able to **re**deem it or buy it back. We can't **re**turn to the store unless we already went to the store. *Romans 12:2* instructs us to be transformed by the **re**newing of our minds. **Re**newing our minds isn't just **re**programming our minds with new information as we get rid of old information. **Re**newing our minds is deeper than that. A person can't **re**new a magazine subscription unless they already had a magazine subscription. The very fact that God told us to **re**new our mind lets us know we already had a certain mind that He was referring to. *Philippians 2:5* says:

Let this mind be in you, which was also in Christ Jesus.

When you are born again, getting the mind of God isn't a very difficult task. You just have to let it be, because when you were born again, you got it back. Each time we read God's Word, it is reminding us of His Voice and the Holy Ghost begins to bring all things to our remembrance, the things that God conversed with us before time began. *1 Corinthians 2:16* tells us "But we have the mind of Christ."

Priestly Anointing

During the anointing service of Old Testament priests who would serve in the Tabernacle of Moses, the priests were anointed with blood and oil on certain parts of their bodies. First, blood was applied to their right ear, right thumb, and right big toe. After the blood, they applied anointing oil to the same areas. (*Exodus 29:20*) The ear represents hearing. The thumb represents the things we touch and hold, and the big toe symbolizes our steps and walk. The order was, first the Blood, then the oil. This is why Calvary came before Pentecost. Christ shed His sinless Blood before God poured out the oil of the Holy Spirit.

First, Jesus *sweat* Blood from His head, and then again shed Blood from His head because of the crown of thorns. As the Blood ran from his brow, it covered His ears. They nailed Him in His hands and feet. When we give our hearts to the Lord, He covers us in His own Blood. It not only washes away our sins, but we are anointed with His Blood for the royal priesthood and are ready for the anointing of His Spirit. We must ask to be filled with His Spirit so the oil of the Spirit can touch our ears, our hands, and our feet, and properly prepare us to be a Holy Priest in this fallen world.

Because Jesus restored us back to headship and has made proper atonement for the healing of our minds through the shedding of His Blood from His head, we have legal access to the mind of Christ. We are now *"bone of His Bone and flesh of His Flesh."* We are no longer strangers and aliens to the Covenant, but we are joint-heirs with Jesus Christ. (**Romans 8:17**) We have the mind of Christ! All we have to do is let it come forth.

Chapter Seven
Goliath's Head

And David took the head of the Philistine; and brought it to Jerusalem...

1 Samuel 17:54

After the famous duel between David and Goliath where David defeated the giant with a sling and a stone and cut Goliath's head off, David did something prophetic when he took the giants head to Jerusalem. Jerusalem was not yet the capital of Israel. It did not become Israel's capital until after David became king and established his headquarters there. David did not take Goliath's body or his amour to Jerusalem, but he only took his head. Why? I believe it is connected to God's prophecy of Genesis 3:15.

And I will put enmity between thee and the woman, and between thy seed and her seed; it shall bruise thy head and thou shalt bruise his heel.

Giants were the offspring of the fallen angels who broke the laws of the universe and married human women. These angels not only lusted for women, but wanted to establish their own family and diabolical bloodline in the Earth to ultimately contaminate human DNA and hinder the promise of the Seed of the woman. Though the flood killed off the original breed of giants, the process was repeated after the flood as evidence of races of giants are seen throughout the promised land, the most infamous being Goliath from Gath. It is interesting that the presence of giants aren't mentioned in scripture after Goliath and his four brothers. David took the head of Goliath to Jerusalem because it signaled the end of its bloodline and fulfillment of scripture.

I believe David took Goliath's head to Jerusalem and hid it inside the hill where Jesus would one day be crucified on. This hill has three names all meaning head. Three is the number of divine testimony and God was really trying to get our attention with the location where salvation would take place. *The place of a skull* could refer to the skull of Goliath that David brought to

Jerusalem. The name Goliath and Golgotha are very similar.

Goliath's head placed by David inside the hill known as the Place of a skull would fulfill God's prophecy of Genesis 3:15 concerning the Seed of the Woman bruising the head of the seed of the serpent. Jesus is the Seed of the woman. Women do no produce seed, men do. Jesus was the Seed of the woman because He was from Heaven and impregnated in the virgin Mary by the Holy Ghost. Giants are fallen seed of the enemy from angelic and human mixture. As Jesus hung on top of Calvary, His feet would be positioned above the head of the hidden skull of Goliath inside the same hill. In essence, having the Seed of the woman (Jesus) whose feet (heel) is above of the head of the seed of the serpent!

1 Peter 3:19 informs us that Jesus preached to the spirits in prison when He died and went to the heart of the Earth for three days and nights. He preached to the angels who took wives of humans and created the abominable race of giants. These angels were banished by God to the lowest and hottest part of hell called

Tartarus. *Jude 1:6* Jesus visited them during His time in Hell to inform them that their strategy to contaminate the bloodline of man did not succeed and His prophecy spoken in the garden of Eden after the fall came to pass. He is the Seed of the woman who had just crushed the head of the seed of the serpent and would soon be resurrected as the Head of the body of Christ.

Luke 19:10 says Jesus came to seek and save that which was lost and it was man's headship that was lost with the fall and on a hill with three names all meaning head, Jesus died for our sins, crushed the head of the enemy and restored us back in relationship with God, paying the price for us to have the mind of Christ. This is the revelation of Calvary.

PRAYER OF SALVATION

Heavenly Father, I come to You admitting that I am a sinner. I choose to turn away from sin, and I ask You to cleanse me from all unrighteousness. I believe Your Son Jesus died so that I may be forgiven of my sins and made righteous through faith in Him. I call upon the Name of Jesus Christ to be my Savior and the Lord of my life. Jesus, I choose to follow You and I ask that You fill me with the power of the Holy Spirit. I declare I am a child of God. I am free from sin and full of the righteousness of God. I am saved. In Jesus' Name. **Amen**.

ABOUT THE AUTHOR

Romel Duane Moore Sr. was born in Chicago, Illinois. He served as Pastor of Liberty Temple Full Gospel Church of Fort Wayne, Indiana for five years. Romel has worked in middle schools, group homes, and served as the Director of the Faith-Based Program, Unity of Love Family Reconnect, helping ex-offenders readjust after being released from prison. He has worked closely with re-entry court programs, serving as a liaison between ex-offenders and re-entry court. Romel has taught in prisons and juvenile facilities in Illinois, Indiana, Ohio, Georgia, and Florida. He has mentored with Big Brothers, Big Sisters and the Boys and Girls Club of America. Romel volunteers with American Red Cross. He has holds crusades, feeds the homeless, and cares for the helpless. He hosted the weekly television Christian program "Keys of the Kingdom." He is owner and Author of PCT Publishing. He is a twenty-year accounting professional. All of Pastor Romel's books are available on Amazon, Kindle, and Createspace. If you desire to have Romel for a speaking engagement you may contact him at (808) 397-4906.

Footnotes

[1] Analogy quote is taken from 2Kings 6:7.

[2] Hawn, Michael History of Hymns: "Nothing but the Blood"
http://www.umcdiscipleship.org/resources/history-of-hymns-nothing-but-the-blood

Made in the USA
Columbia, SC
11 September 2024

42105160R00037